Asleep in the
Lightning Fields

Jorn Ake

Winner, X. J. Kennedy Poetry Prize, 2001

Texas Review Press
Huntsville, Texas

First Edition, 2002

Requests for permission to reproduce material from this work
should be sent to

> Permissions
> Texas Review Press
> English Department
> Box 2146
> Sam Houston State University
> Huntsville, TX 77341-2146

Acknowledgments

Apostrophe: "Death of a Tractor's Son," "Chicken Fried Steak"

The Mochila Review (formerly *Icarus*): "Push Mower Heavenly
  Body," "Egg Bound Cowboy Blues," "How My Wife Saves the
  Day"

I would like to thank my teachers, Beckian Fritz Goldberg, Norman
Dubie, Jeannine Savard, and Alberto Rios, for being incredible insti-
gators of great poetry. I would also like to thank Ruth Ellen Kocher
and Mary Boyes, who read my bad poetry and helped make it better.
And I would like to thank Salima Keegan and Karla Elling, both of
whom offered invaluable support to many writers at ASU, myself in-
cluded. And finally, I thank my wife, Claudia, for her patience and
perseverance.

Library of Congress Cataloging-in-Publication Data

Ake, Jorn, 1964-
    Asleep in the lightning fields / Jorn Ake.-- 1st ed.
        p. cm.
    ISBN 1-881515-44-3 (alk. paper)
    I. Title
    PS3601.K39 A93 2002
    811'.6--dc21
                                            2002005123

For Claudia,

without whom I would be impossible

Table of Contents

3

Ignorant of the water I go seeking
a death full of light to consume me.
—Gabriel Garcia Lorca

Hauling the Dead Horse

You hook the hoof with a loop
tied to the hitch of the tractor
and drag him from the pasture
to the barn.

Even though you know he is dead
and it doesn't really matter anymore
you think about the skin scraped off
from the dark underside and wonder
where it goes.

This wonder makes you a little proud
before you enter the barn
thinking the tractor was something
you could start and that it had
a hook and would pull.

Gray Dipper Song

Plump, short-tailed birds; resemble large wrens.
Solitary. Dive, swim underwater, walk on the bottom.
                              —A Field Guide to Western Birds

The creek is distant, clacks
rocks like syllables—

water's voice, a mother
turned away
from a lighted kitchen window.

I stumble down a moss greased bank,
the cows deep
in it, sleeping standing,

a shoulder against the almost-dark.

I must have been here
before I ever was.

A dipper, head beneath a wing,
one foot, sings
an underwater nightingale.

Trout hold the bottom
against their ears,
to listen—

see fish the surface, see
the chortled world woven above
on a loom gray shadow.

I am the bobbin, I am the shuttle.

Sometimes, in deep water, I consider rising
not the inevitable sun.

Push Boat Morning Blues

The aluminum boat chunging through brown water
runs a school of shad
from the shadow of a Clorox bottle float.

The hook nabs the yellow rope
and scrapes a crab pot
over the gunwales,
dumping four or five blue crab
into the boat's mid-section.

Usually the fog is light.
Usually the water skiers are not up
yet.

Mellifluous is just a word
for sorting crabs by,

the dead flung upward and shattered
by a shotgun's blast.

Each shot
like a conversation with God
unanswered

pushes the anchorless boat
a little farther into the weeds.

Photograph: Norfolk, VA 1969

Here's the one that looks like me.
I seem to be working a pump
into a basketball,
deflated and waiting.

I think I needed to make a world
small enough to fit comfortably
on a front porch brightened by sun,

large enough a tired-faced child
could have a place to hover above.

So I am beginning to make my little world,
in this bent-up photo, here.

Look, thirty years run along the bottom,
staining the linoleum
with cheap appliance rust,

and the air comes in acrid puffs
through a decrepit window screen.

But the bent boy calls out like a boxed calf,
my thumb on something like its heart-

in the picture, gray on gray on gray.

Learning to Tie My Own Shoes

The sun is rising and the light has the clarity of vodka. Leaves slightly removed from the trees. A breeze. The bus stop sign is not new. My mother bends to tie my shoes. She makes two knots. After twenty years, I remember this. First one knot. Tighten. Then the second knot. Tighter. She does not stand. She does not walk away.

Might Have Been That Tractor

for Bill

About my family, there once was an uncle
like my father.

It makes sense that he is gone.
But a certain tension stays
and I often have to stand
at the backyard fence
and watch the neighbor's dog.

Even as a dog, my uncle refuses me,
yet his hold is unbroken
and exceeds his size.

I need to get to him.
I need a word for tractor
that is red enough and smells
like a hand
on metal touching plastic.

The plastic is on fire.
A man could be on the tractor.

Done is good he said
and he got down
to stand with me at the fence.
He said the dog told him
a dead uncle can go on
and on like a brother.
Then the tractor's smell

or the plastic's fire
could be done
but not both.

Lost Love of Scissors

She asked you about it.
Your smile fell
marionette awkward,
loosed from its strings
by the silver scissors mother kept
in the special drawer

you were not allowed
to open without permission.

At night you could hear the scissors sing.
How alone silver can be.

In the morning, you longed to run
down the block
out along the dangerous bulkheads
above the polluted river.
You wanted to run with scissors.

Only then could there be any talk
of marriage.

Broadcast on a Brown Radio

In this case, a boxing match—

sitting on a wooden bench
before the fight, the boxer
sweats too heavily.
Leans a shoulder into the wall
to click on the dusty brown radio
stowed darkly on its shelf.

Tonight, he will hear a song
that reminds him of a girl
who was something like his mother
when he was young,

out in the garden
tossing seed by the handful
from a paper bag,

her back turned
towards the open gate.

Cut Blue Skin

I ran into the well-lit bathroom and slipped, the blue skin of my forehead cut so deep I heard you inhale so not to let go. I told you I listened when you slept. How you breathed in, then paused. I imagined the moment as a loss like the last box mislaid at Christmas. Then found. A new red truck. A ticking watch I could hold in my hand. I would have traded you for anything. My blood flowed like sleep. Our house was nearly empty beside its dry river bed.

Love Song For My Cello

Understand, the bus is Jonah's whale
I entered long ago.

The boy who sat on the bus
had a cello in his hand.
A man staggered up
with his hand out.

The boy rocked on this cliff's edge
like a murre's egg, sky blue
fingers clutching
his sweet cello-wife.

Don't touch me.

The ethical thing was to feel
like a bed at night—a tenderness bed
stacked with newspaper clippings,
stories of people
who honestly do the wrong thing.

The boy and this feeling of knowing
kicked the svelte back
of his cello
with something like love—

a brown shoe, worn at the toe
one lace tattered,
slightly untied.

A Flattened Ball

The grass waited patiently
on the season to turn
the boy green,
color him alone and holy
like the dead mother's writing
on the cardboard box in the attic
a ball was tossed into-

a keepsake, a memento
detached from its love.

The season became whatever happened
and green simply meant to be green,

never the shade
the boy ran from
with skinned knees
and sloppy socks tensioned
with rubber bands.

He came in late from the dark.
He held it tightly in his hands
so it would not be lost.

Chicken Fried Steak

      is a thing I have not witnessed
myself, that and the making
of tapioca pudding,
I said to the waitress
at a counter in Koscuisko,
Mississippi.
Made their own donuts too,
everything greased stickiness
like the tar-bandaged handle of a bat
after the full count
and a single to right.
Nothing much to all of it,
just hot water
and a box of those pearls you get
at the grocer's.
The spring on the screen groaned
the breeze of fans
belted to a motor out back.
I said ma'am
just to hear the way she said
Puhrrls
with the—uh of slow humping
the—url of Earl. Distant
as a photograph I was not part of,
a woman, a counter, dark
thumb print on the white border,
folded and lost in a pocket.
She wiped a table, counted
the change in her tip,
oily rag in her hand singing
circle be unbroken.

The Death of a Tractor's Son

If I ever see that white light
That comes up the back of the head
And lays out all sides of everything,
I'll lay down my tools.
I'll walk away.
        —farmer, rt. 5, Charles City County, Virginia

I couldn't see him
in the light dust of the bathroom.
There was just the one lamp
leaning in from the lost backyard.
I could only feel that he had come.
He lifted, one arm under each of mine
muscles bent and worn smooth with the weight
of walking and bending and grasping.
There was no suddeness to his breath,
no crack of sinews pulling against his bones
as he braced his feet, his back.
I knew he had been plowing all day,
field smell in his hands,
the tractor and its bent steering rod
left idling, only half the soy beans done.
I knew he would be tired.
Still I fell and could not move.
I could not see his sweat, the hay in his hatband,
a red cloth lain over his scalp.
Could not recall the softness of the heart's press
to the holes of my ears, or remember
how the flutter of the lungs began. Slowly
he gathered the bones of my shoulders
raising what was me to the edge of the stairs,
and then out to the field,

laying me the length of its deepest furrow,
arms together, hands reaching,
wrists turned inward,
the darkness of sweet corn
bending down to hiss
take me home.

What Becomes of Distance

driving from Los Angeles to Phoenix

When there are no longer any people
there will still be pigeons,
leaping from the stone of a bridge.

Underneath will be all the water.

What does sand do when it is all the same?
Flattens, then erodes
along made-up lines of difference.

A fence post, separated from its kind,
gathers a little around the base
for comfort and stability.
Twenty years later, a mountain.

At this point, I wasn't looking.

350 miles had come as close as possible
to endlessness,
stood on tiptoe, peeked
over the windowsill of my long black car.

I had to park, get out,
stare into the desert.

It was enough
and all so necessary—
the unnecessary shrinking
like nylon in flame.

I wanted to be part
of the shimmering lake on a highway

that rises as one
with what disappears.

This Poem Was Always about Anger

A cigarette's blood end, poppy
grown from your lips—

call me a taxi rolled beneath
the heaviest crush of roses.

No one will find my body there.

As a boy, I saw movies.

I always wanted to ride
the flaming bus down the gorge
and explode on the canyon floor
below

like a carnation afire,

the saved
perched on the overlook thinking
first the skin then
the bones and then, at last,
the teeth.

We are Rolled in a Dog like a World

Speed and sleep have overlapped. My body,
Sack for eternity.
                    —Norman Dubie

1.

My car falls through a spigot of rain
as the wipers smear the windshield.
Each set of oncoming lights
blinds me until I am alone
with the dark, the page of a book
crushed to the floor boards
between the accelerator and brake.
It tells how the story will go—
there'll be a couple people,
one will die, another will live
with a squeaky, black little lie.
It'll all be in first-person.

2.

I have belted the typewriter
into the passenger's seat,
so I can write anytime I drive.
I spilled hot coffee
on my lap at three a.m.
when a voice came in the dark
and my hands closed tightly around—
why come to the kitchen table
wrapped in southern light, robe fallen
open as if open meant ready,

belly white as trout skin
slit for the red breakfast roe.

3.

The dog is gnawing the platen.
After four hours of banging, typewriter
against house, he's finally gotten somewhere.
He gets this way when he's been drinking.
By noon we'd finished the first bottle.
Then he asked for cigarettes.
Then he asked for the typewriter.
Wrote a short poem about the heartache
a dog feels for what's buried beneath.
This morning, he came grinning
to the screen door, an arm crossways
in his mouth.

The Blind De Soto

A glass plate grays
in the grip of an old car
lost to flat land—

my hand across your mouth.

What emptiness held
that hole in the ground misshapen
could not contain the sound.

The chair's scrape in an evaporated room.
Chain wrenched from a winch.

Dominican, this broken frame house,
curl of yellow paper undusted
by a forefinger lingering.

A child's skull parched
by six months of desert,

sockets clumped with skin—

among the natives, I drink
laudanum from its cap, lie
without need for embellishment.

With water, I made them all
my children of God.

My Student Writes of My Death

Let the Day perish wherein I was Born.
                              —Job 3:3

I have considered this pipe
which runs from the furnace
to my wooden room.
It curves like the neck of a man
cut down from a tree.

He painted the forest behind the refrigerator
in blue mold and coffee.
Then ate his last poem, washed down
with anti-freeze from a lidless jar.

His neighbors found him stiff and folded.

I hear boat horns swim up from the river,
the tugs working against the flow.

They stole his box-crates of notes
to re-kindle the wood stove,
then wrapped him in torn linen
and tied his feet with clothesline
to an oak plank from his bed.

Yesterday, I received a small silver flask
from a friend. Its eloquence
chills me, perched as it is
on the opened window sill.

On a patch of ceiling
sketched in shaky pencil,

irrelevant
was pressed into soft plaster
nine times in a row.

But, lifted to the lips, its river pours
strangely and I am a raft cut adrift...

A brown paper bag stashed in a brick chink
held the current
rent.

Careful Singing

It's a list of what I cannot touch.
                              —Larry Levis

Yesterday, I found the skeleton
of an Inca dove killed by a cat.

I put a hole in each bone,
strung them together on a strand
of white cotton waxed yellow
by the sun.

The pull cord from the shed—

I wonder why we connect
light to dark by a thread
dangled from the rafters above?

I cannot reach the light anymore.

Is this when I should hum nervously to myself?

There may be two answers here: I do not
and I do not at all.

How come when I am alone,
everything is nighttime
and so fucking beautiful
I cry like there is no tomorrow.

And then tomorrow
I say Now.   Now.
A wholly hollow sound.

Another Night Gets It in the End

How long can the same thing be done
before any dance floor
becomes any factory
and any factory

the timeclock beneath
every overpass.

There are coffee cans.
Dog pens. Parking lots.

A little story ticking.

There was the one street lamp
and its puddle of work—

a man's burred hand held
against a woman in a dress.

Then the sun
brought its own.

All things rose
with the sigh
electricity throws
across the room to the dark.

Mandelstam in Virginia

I sit in the open hospital window,
the ground calling out *leap*
louder than the cardinals
in the tangled greenbriar below.

If I am alive at the bottom,
they will carry me back inside
and tape me hard to a bed.

There is a smudge on the wall
where I put all that was lost.

I still cannot see
how to make it end.

In this book is a photograph—

the fish from the jungle stream
that enters the rectum
and cannot be removed.

How does it know?
Why does it stop?

Sunken Deadrise in an Estuary

The mourning dove lies
on the gray pine of a wreck
scuttled here, half raised,
half sunk down in the silt,

like a bull on his knees,
head bowed, willing his back legs
to understand a blow of the sledge,
when there is only the breath
and a subtle click.

The dove with a small wet spot
on the breast, rows one wing,
its eye over my shoulder,
opening the sky.

A good deadrise can only be sunk
with a load of sand, a box
of shotgun shells and an axe.

In the hull, I count twelve holes—

part of it all, to keep afloat,
then sink when time comes
and asks why one more time.

Can there only be a rest,
a pause—

I shot the dove because
the girl with one lung staggered

to the piano, touched

one note rising

and one note
breathing

the dove instead.

Whence I Came

The incessant and terminal gardening
that we all do—

the dead dog on the freezer
coughed a halo of sodium pentathol
while my back was turned.

This was my shelter job.
The dying was not finished.

I waited with a green trash bag
and its twist-tie in my hand,

not one thing anymore, but grown
and split in two.

Small Wooden Elegy

When an infant dies in Toraja
a tree's bark is folded back,
the body is slipped inside.
Sutures pull the soft wood together
to swallow the bones,
draw the small hands in.

Slowly, the child becomes the side of the tree.
A mound remains.

A heaven turned over
in a curled thumb—

a wound to reach in
and take your other side.

2

And then the fire comes, and then the shadow,
and who knows which is which?
—Michael Burkard

Lost Snail Song

When sleep comes hard as an ingot of onyx
the old shoes sit by the back door,
their sandy foot beds and cupped soles
familiar with the bend
of kneeling beside the fountain.

Snails circle there in the slime.
I carry a pencil to trace their steps
in graphite dust across shiny trails,
a cartographer's rough sketches
of slippery places clearly imagined.

Here a coastline marauds an open field
that sleeps fitfully behind a wall
that runs along a silver road
that lies beneath an early moon
that leads eventually to a surface
more familiar to the touch,

with an even brown and a window
and the yellow of a single lamp
spinning somewhere deep inside.
A body waits there for a hand,

the touch of a hand,
but feels only the absence of feet
unfurling slowly in the textured darkness.

Plastic Coffee Cup

I used to go over there just to hear
the spring on her screen door go twang.

The pile of dishes in the sink
and the work boots muddy
from the garden
showed the way to the body within.

This isn't the strongest *mea culpa*.
There was an illegal relationship
before the final cup of coffee—

debris accompany any sing along.

Occasionally, a cramp
or sudden fatigue stops the melody.
Or a plastic bag gets sucked
into the mouth
preventing future respiration.
The subject is left gasping
and blue as a favorite mug.

Later, you hold the dirt from digging
in the lines of your hand
and must remember to wash up
alone each morning before you leave.

The flowers at the back gate waving
out of the bed beyond empty and cold.
Little boundaries for ourselves to cross
and find the silver kitchen spoon
clumped with compost and slugs.

Secret Snapshot

Weather came in the back door
as the other woman asking
"if I made the noise
a heavy woolen coat
would it hold me to you?"

My wife was on the right.
I disappeared slowly
into the dark night between
a coffin of hastily driven nails
and the loose board in the porch.

Rain pestered the ground
until the dirt divided
soft as skin beneath a knife.

My wife stood still,
her hand on the switch.
She said the word *two*
was the moth we made.

It went crazy with light.

The Girl Who Sailed Like Kites

First there is something not stupid
or imaginary, just there
in the skin, the thorn pushed
through a leather glove—

planting chollas in rows
to keep away the cats
who kill the doves and shit
behind the garage.

No why to them.
Just because.

The dead doves left open like books
about nothing
are as beautiful
as the small piece of blanket
beneath the knee of a girl
whose name I remember

as a language. As if

this atmosphere, this memory
goes through everything

like the spine in my palm.

I need to grow a plant.
I need to push the shovel down
but feel nothing.
A wingless carcass flies

stronger than this life.

How can it?

Ask me. Ask me
what about the girl.
She sailed like kites.

Asleep in the Lightning Fields

I pass your house in the big field
and hear the earth grow still inside me.

A train runs empty from the bridge,
noteless as a sun-blued bottle
and its porous *oh*.

The clouds blacken and crack
into smaller pieces,

torn photographs

each stuck once with a silver straight pin
then buried beneath the field's fescue.

Listen, these bristle dry grasses name us—
he loved the horse in her hair,
the early fire-storm . . .

All that was needed was a match
and its sweet flower alcohol
to lay the grassland bare.

My hand's blue spark
over your darkened head
as lightning released
by the ground's pull—

somewhere a pasture
filled with metal rods
burns as brightly

in blackness,
each electified hole filled
with memories lost.

Have I never been here?
Have I ever been

asleep in a crush of sage?

Wheat folds beneath
the weight of rain.

A city explodes.

Above, your hollow-sweet song
spins.

Alcohol

It was when all I wanted was a silver mirror to put in my pocket, to take out and kill Distance without turning to stone, that her sweet sisters, weeping gin and lime, came up behind me and would not go away.

My Wife Drives the Car Through the Flower Bed While Going in Reverse: Part 1

I showed the clouds how to cover up the clear blue sky.
—Johnny Cash

I lie in my backyard of grass seed,
with the word *digitalis* on my lips
and an arm outstretched,
shaking slightly
to scare away starlings and thrashers.
The grass seed sings
there is a man in the backyard
so wonderfully I dream of him
and of his furniture—
a nice desk made of metal,
a soap dish, a towel rack.
It is a happy dream.
I do not expect
this man will die
or that the birds will eat him
and the grass seed
should he sleep here too long.
I expect my wife will arrive
and I will get up,
death loosed from me
with a wave of her hand.

Behind Maggie's Grocery

Not one to try on small things
I wrapped resurrection in a shirt—

one hundred percent Holy Roller cotton
with those dancing Baby Jesus cufflinks.

Only the best for my baby.
I heard that once on the radio,
said like a man on fire—

he said the proof is in how
you handle your tools.

I prefer the hammer and shovel routine
out behind the five and dime.

But where I got resurrection
and where I put it afterwards
are two different things.

On visiting days, I take a path
through sand that moves
like water

a way so beautiful
it licks my arm at night
and weeps.

I Was a Teen-Age Summer Camp

At the summer camp, sweet permission
hangs out behind the wooden showers—

naked boys
and girls in clothes full of holes.

The boys get out their touch
and finger each hole,
until no one sees the hand
in front of their face.

You can play the camp counselor
who stumbles from the tent
drunk from a dream of heavy cream
and slivered Georgia peaches,
confused by this small pornography
wriggling like a heart out-of-the-body,
the lung out of a fish.

No field guide at your disposal
lists such an animal,
nor does your first aid kit
have the particular elliptical bandage
required for its pain.

The heartbeats are the boys.
The subtle breathing is the girls,
a rising hip, leg, inner thigh
seen by an unseen hand.
At first sight of you,
they scatter like quail,

then call softly to each other
from the bushes.

This sound helps them return.
You are lost without it.

Kelvinator Moon

Ultimately, the light was falling,
was a motion like a sand dollar
wavering away from

where the refrigerator leans,

safekeeping out of the rain
beneath the thundering eaves
of the wrecked garage.

No food is interested
in entering a place
like this.

With poultry everywhere, even I am
tired.

The woman (I will call her
Opaline) leans over the fence
saying Opaline, my efflorescence

why wander like a Cadillac.

In a flash, I see what she is
talking about—

then light closes
and I am left waiting in darkness
for a luminous non sequitur
to pull back the lever.

Why My Garage Talks Slowly

I say the piñata of fear that hangs in my garage
lies about the quality of my ordinary lawn.

My wife says it is a coffee can
stuffed full of photographs—
me standing open-mouthed,
me arm in arm, me cheek to brilliant cheek.

There are bottles in each
that tell tales I wrote,
though I've forgotten which is which.

I remember one where I ran madly
from the house, slamming the screen door.
The neighbor's infant screamed
like the lamb of Abraham.

God said in his chuckling voice
beyond the last steps of a field
there is always a dog
barking at a man drinking.

I say in my garage is a ghost
I killed with a chunk of brick.

I strapped it to a chair
and bashed it
with unnecessary joy.

Fire Sermon at a Burnt-Out Gas Station

for Ben

Last week, a guy got shot.
Then the gas station burned.

The afterlife is straw-yellow.

Flames split the garage doors.
Water washed the chalk away.

A low full moon like a waiting room.

All that was left
was a concrete darkness.

Say something by which we are saved.

My neighborhood buries their stories
in the soft mud of a river's bank.

What is the smallest story you can tell.

The gas station was on fire. The fire
was just like a picture of a gas station
throwing darkness into an emptying sky.

No, smaller.

Once there was a body and then
there was the outline of a body
washed away.

Smaller.

The next morning, I found casings strewn
like periwinkle shells at low tide.

No.

The next morning, I woke up.
The outside was bright enough to see.

My flower boxes bloomed.
There was a cold morning yellow sun.

Missing a Piece of Praise

Assholes chase one another
off the freeway.
I can hear them yell out
whatever comes to mind.

I have a dining room table.
It's round and over-sanded
with a couple substantial legs.

I praise this table.
The side has a crack,
missing a piece.
I have an open window
to demonstrate its quality.

Six paperwhite bulbs
unplanted in the center.

I can't finish things
I remember ending badly.

The yelling goes on
unmentioned by neighbors.

I do the laundry.

All the socks need new shoes.
I try to give the socks
a good folding over.
The yelling centers the open window.

I pummel what clothes see
as no better day
to be a loose bra strap
and a dress like a curtain.

I pummel what yells in the space
between houses and fences.

I pummel you, brother,
drawn from the freeway
to this crack in my table,
my single sock of truth.

What Entirely Light

The spot electricity enters a building
is like a brown dog

head in a hole looking.
I'm a rabbit.

High as a kite
on carrots.

A rabbit kite
held at the end
of a very long string
by a carrot.

Plug me into the brown dog.

I want this lightness.
I want that light.

Black Secret Dog

As a boy, we all lay wondering
if the door would open
and we would be let go.

Somewhere parents swam in the flame
at the end of a match, breathing
all the air a house could contain
while the golem beneath the bed nibbled
our finger tips.

We thought black secret dog,
light enough to eat birds
and pulled the whiteness of sheets
neck high.

The doorknob aglint in the middle
of an early morning we sang to:

Door, door, let me be a reaching hand
turning into you.

Little animal in the bed swelling
into a fearful boy, wrapped
and waiting for everything to open.

Now, I lie here, naked and unsheeted,
having found a way to swallow the boy
without raising suspicion,

my arms bravely swinging below
what I fear now—
  not dog or bird

Night in the Desert During the Drought

The snakes that hid beneath the sink
were desperate for water.

We put them in pillow cases
and had a vision of each other as two
carrying halves of our own copulation
from the house sheeted and writhing.

There was a blue flame leaping
between the mountains to the west.

Everything was coming and going in circles.

We took a snapshot of us
leaving the house
with this moment in hand
and its snakes
to hold onto the feeling
of an unmet love turning over and over

before the rain moved in
and washed the dried corpse of a pigeon
from beneath the car into the street

to be swallowed slowly down
the gullet of inevitably rising waters
that come from a storm in parched land.

The Pretty Black Flower Dream

It comes and goes like a nipple
and gets written down occasionally
in smudgy pencil
and sounds kind of tickly
when I sing it loud.

My wife confuses me
with the singer
and drives me to the ballroom
for the auditions.

In my dream, the microwave,
the stereo, the television
operate simultaneously.

This occurs in reality too,
just before we leave.

Strapped into the passenger's seat
I begin to believe
I can win the auditions.
It was once a dream of mine
when I was small and asleep.

Egg Bound Cowboy Blues

When I close my eyes, I see a chicken
in a small cage
who loves me.

When I open them, the car is in the driveway.
The cooling engine pings like rain
on the deadpan backyard of Bermuda stubble.

My good eye sits in the left part
of the rear view mirror.
Comfort stands in the right,
the shape of the backdoor
to the house—

my bad eye like a dark pebble caught
in the brown shoe of my head
wanders away,

sullen hands stuffed into its pockets.

I like to remember the click on the radio
as the chicken
and 10,000 singing cowboys who hum

I find I too am slipping
through chain-link fences
with nothing but sky to hold me down.

I Left a Garage Behind Me

Once there was a beautiful liquid
that flowed in greens as though it were
yellow effluent from a blue lemon.

Now there is something squashed
beneath the tire of a car
on a vacant desert highway.

To the East is a deserted photograph
of a house, the flames of saltmarsh
in the distance.

The sun is parafin and gasoline.

We dozed our way out here,
through pages and pages
of *The Plants of the Southwest*,
scratched the latin names out
in the ash of a creosote fire in August.

I am told this movement
is more or less like a broken heart,
like something plastic, broken
like a heart.

When I left, an important flower
waved steadily from the black
window of the wooden garage.

Only then did I see
the shake in my empty hand.

Mumbling the Family Hymnal

I am really into the smart pop song
right now, forgetting

the one with the words
we all used to sing as kids

My baby herrumm zah ta you
yeah oh uhhmmm duh you oh

brings back the memories of a sister
and what's-his-name
dancing urgently in vague swimsuits,

my sullen period of ruined jukeboxes,
and the steak house cataclysm.

The funny part was the sound
I made out of the squeeze box
we buried mother in.

Oh baby yer uhm ruff mmmmm she sang

with a lushness
I drank (I thought)
to cure myself of past sickness.

But what I really did
was avoid the song
or the sound of the song
or my mother singing
and then me craftily singing
alone.

New Kitchen Gospel Music

I found my wife with my own hands
sewn into the pockets of an apron.

It was beautiful this way.
The apron flowing out towards the sea.

Even the audience was moist and tender,
cradling and swaying
like a chorus in a country church
after the singing had stopped
and the stomping and the clapping.
Then all the praying out loud
Amen shaking the white paint
off the clapboards and my wife
looking up at me

or the bright sky behind me
or the bird flying diagonally
as it unraveled the thread
to weave into a nest cup

in a way familiar
to the sigh an apron makes
as it enters the sea
and begins to sing.

The audience is as quiet as a fried egg.

Push Mower Heavenly Body

The household man steps into the blooms
next to the hose and the spigot
with the swagger of an aging swinger.
He remembers the television
still warm in the house
and resolves to touch the push mower
before the day ends.
He feels this will be something
of which he can be proud
and carry with him in a pocket
like a secret ball
snipped from its selfish paddle.
There is freedom loose in the garden.
To be this ball and lie face up
on the cool floor of the garage.
There is another thing to be
in a crinkled photo
the man keeps quietly to himself.
This can be the theme for the day.
A theme can make anyone happy.
It can be like the first breath
after the sufficient mint dissolves.
It can be like the light oil
found unexpectedly
on the dark spot the tongue touched
beneath the twirling blades
rolling over and over in the grass.

Gardening Provençal

Charlemagne's house leeks
pudgy with misbegotten water
bask among the flagstones
like a holiday of bathers.

I am not here to kill anyone.

In the garden, I am with my plants
unconserved as a dirty relic.
I have my coffee before the sun is hot,
the sprinkler's residue on the lip
of the blue glazed pot by the backdoor
where I sit.

I am not what I seem.

Just the thin silver flash
of the trowel loosening the grip
on one errant aloe after another.

The path was here once before.
It takes only a quiet morning of steady work
to bring its surface to light once again.

Why Bulbs in the Desert

The book is portly in its paper cover,
full of bulbs and lilies
with no business in a desert garden.

Still I go out into it,
pages curling in the heat
as I fold over corners,
make notes in the margins
about the location of shade
and ground temperature
with a broken pencil
dropped while clapboarding the garage.

A finger smudge sticks to an alium,
its flower a glorious softball,
the bulb all fat onion.

At noon, I am thin in the sun
and leave little shadow.
I love what I lack.

I order it from the east coast
and plant it in the dry soil
spaced every six and a half inches.

Clementine, My Pruning Shears

You make offering emphatic advice to plants
easier, yellow-rubber handled.
Lost in tall grass or
pocketed in the pocket of my pants,
you talk ideas with bedroom eyes
that say a snack is in order—
snip-snip, snip-snip.

Meet me at the hummingbird confessional.
We'll watch the throats move like
a regular hundred hands swallowing.
I'm desperate for that sort of ecstasy
in this topiary, that desert broom—
portable potableness with a slight twist
of citrus—Oh Clementine

how come your teeth are so big?
You make me forget the look on my face.
You make me forget the pleasure
of grinding a pencil to dust.

How My Wife Saves the Day

My wife says, little brick, wake up.
I make some coffee
and put on my pants
for one more day.

She says, my cow, paper's here.
I drink my coffee
and spend too much time
on an article about dung beetles.

She says, sweet, backyard's on fire.
I go outside
and stand in the center.

These are my flowers, I say,
red as they are
they are you.

I am your wife, she says, wave,
wave for my red camera.

My Wife Drives The Car Through The Flower Bed While Going in Reverse: Part 2

I feel myself harden with the landscape.

—Robert Desnos

There's more.
A distinct feeling the clouds
are not moving.
A way to avoid any happy ending
with care.

After years twisted tightly,
I loosen
to find the desire
to say everything
will be alright

drives through the penstemon,
embarrassed by the sweetness
of its demise.

3

Riding beside me, your seat belt around your invisible waist.
Sweet
Nothing.
Sweet, sweet nothing.
- Larry Levis

Lullaby for a Young Road

At day's end, I lie down
like a quiet path.
I say my name before I sleep,
once secretly,
and once to my path
so that it may remember my location.
Little traveler, I say, *when I wake,*
carry me like a lamb to my name.